Eiry Shepherd

Cottingham
in old picture postcards

by
K.R. Green
and
E.M. Green

European Library - Zaltbommel/Netherlands MCMLXXXVI

GB   ISBN 90 288 3346 3 / CIP

©1986 European Library - Zaltbommel/Netherlands

European Library in Zaltbommel/Netherlands publishes among other things the following series:

IN OLD PICTURE POSTCARDS *is a series of books which sets out to show what a particular place looked like and what life was like in Victorian and Edwardian times. A book about virtually every town in the United Kingdom is to be published in this series. By the end of this year about 175 different volumes will have appeared. 1,250 books have already been published devoted to the Netherlands with the title* **In oude ansichten.** *In Germany, Austria and Switzerland 500, 60 and 15 books have been published as* **In alten Ansichten;** *in France by the name* **En cartes postales anciennes** *and in Belgium as* **En cartes postales anciennes** *and/or* **In oude prentkaarten** *150 respectively 400 volumes have been published.*

For further particulars about published or forthcoming books, apply to your bookseller or direct to the publisher.

This edition has been printed and bound by Grafisch Bedrijf De Steigerpoort in Zaltbommel/Netherlands.

INTRODUCTION

Cottingham, claimed by its inhabitants as 'the largest village in England', is an ancient parish in the Wapentake of Harthill (South Hunsley Beacon Division). It lies in low flat ground between the Yorkshire Wolds and the river Hull. Newland and Dunswell are now ranked as separate ecclesiastical parishes, but historically the total area of the parish was 9,831 acres. By a Local Government Order of 5th December 1879 a part of the parish of Skidby known as 'Skidby Ings' was added to Cottingham parish. In 1935 Cottingham Urban District ceased to exist, as many local parishes in an attempt to resist absorption by their powerful neighbour Kingston-upon-Hull amalgamated to form the urban district known as Haltemprice — a reference to the ancient priory founded there in 1324 in the village of Newton, two miles south of Cottingham. Haltemprice survived successfully until the reorganisation of local government in 1974 when it entered the County of North Humberside (Beverley Borough District).

Cottingham is a place of considerable antiquity, although it does not come into prominence until the Norman Conquest. There have been many guesses as to the etymology of the name, but a likely derivation is the ham or settlement of the Cottings or Cotta's folk. The Domesday Book 1086, lists the manor for taxes, but an older evidence of habitation was the discovery in the 1860's of four gold bracelets, now in the 'Gold Room' at the British Museum and estimated to be over 2,000 years old.

Domesday Book shows that there were two manors involved, Cottingham and Pileford (the latter name surviving only as the corruption 'Pillwoods'). At that time the manor was in the lordship of Hugh, son of Baldric, with connections in Normandy and was valued at £7. The name most associated with the manor of Cottingham is that of the de Stutevilles. William de Stuteville (about 1140) was granted a charter for a weekly market in 1197 and a licence to build a double moated and palisaded castle. Of this castle (Baynard Castle) only the mound and evidences of the outer moat remain and the market was recently refounded in 1985 on the Market Green. Eventually in 1241, on the death of the lord without male heirs, the manor passed via the heiress Joan into the Wake family and Earls of Kent, by marriage. Joan is seen on a surviving Great Seal, riding side-saddle on a horse — the first illustration of this mode of riding by a woman.

Thomas, Lord Wake, a notable member of the family, for seventeen years constantly in the wars of Edward II and Edward III was granted a further charter by the latter monarch for a market and permission to further fortify his castle. He died in 1349 leaving no male heirs and the manor passed via his daughter Joan Plantagenet (the Fair Maid of Kent) to Thomas Holland. Their eldest son became Baron Wake and Earl of Kent and the manor was held by the Hollands until 1407, when there being again no male heirs it was divided into the separate Manors of Richmond, Sarum, Westmoreland and Powis after the names of the lords who acquired them by marriage with the heiresses. Joan Plantagenet had a second husband, Edward the Black Prince, on the death of her first husband, so that the Plantagenets became involved with the estates during the troubled times of the Wars of the Roses and eventually by 1500 the lands passed into the ownership of the Crown.

Much that was old in the village has disappeared, particularly during the orgy of redevelopment in the 1960's. Fine Georgian houses were demolished to make way for housing estates, to house the growing population of a dormitory town and particularly one so conveniently placed to the new University of Hull, originally established as a University

College in 1927 and granted University status on 13th May 1954. The emphasis had now changed; Cottingham had long been popular as a residential area for wealthy business men such as the Wilsons of shipping fame, lawyers, solicitors, bankers and members of the professions and now it was to become popular as a haven for academics, students and members of the middle classes generally.

Two student halls of residence established before the war in the early years of the college, after granting of the Charter in 1954 gradually grew into a large campus to the north-west of the village. Many of the old houses of the gentry which would have fallen to the developers, were saved and purchased by the University to serve as additional halls and schools. For this the inhabitants of Cottingham should be grateful!

The great increase in population from 1,927 in 1801 to an estimated 18,000 in the 1980's (16,365 in 1971 census) has involved the building of vast estates around the original village. Much of the overspill population originates from the building of mass estates to house families from the nearby City of Kingston-upon-Hull as part of the post-war demolition of terrace dwellings in the city area, but it also embraces the creation of 'executive style' complexes such as that based at Castle Park.

Cottingham is therefore a well-mixed community full of bustle and energy, but nevertheless it has not lost its old charm when one wanders down the main shopping area of Hallgate. Cottingham's pride undoubtedly is the Church of St. Mary the Virgin arguably built between the years 1316 and 1416. As the rectors date from the twelfth century the present building is obviously not the first one on the site. There is no trace of an earlier church although some re-used stone may be present in the nave. In a part of the country famous for such churches as the King of Holderness (at Hedon) and the Queen (at Patrington), Cottingham is worthy of comparison, with its fine commanding tower and the sheer beauty of its chancel. Much of Cottingham's history during the Plantagenet period was portrayed in the heraldic glass of the chancel before the wanton destruction of the civil war.

Nicholas de Luda (Louth) received his living here from Edward the Black Prince — the advowson was owned by his wife Joan Plantagenet, who first married Thomas Holland. He was Cottingham's most famous priest and the creator of the fabulous rebuilt chancel; that Edward III held him in high regard is evident by his reference to Nicholas as 'our beloved clark Nicholas of Louth'. St. Mary's suffered somewhat from the zeal of the Victorian restorers and the Reverend C. Overton was responsible for the lifting of the church floor, thereby shortening the majesty of the pillars and for the demolition of the priests room above the South Porch.

The pictures included in this book largely show what has gone in the village, mainly in post-war years. In some areas changes have taken place without total destruction i.e. in adaptation of old houses as flats or student houses. We are greatly indebted to earlier photographers such as Mr. H.J. Tadman, postmaster at the turn of the century, and commercial suppliers such as Messrs. Frith and Scott. We would like to express our gratitude to many friends and members of the Cottingham Local History Society for permission to reproduce postcards and in particular to Mr. Harry Wright, Mr. Norman Bisby and the late Mrs. Ellen C. Brace for their invaluable help in building up a pictorial record of Cottingham during pre-war years. Our grateful thanks also to Miss Mary Ansdell for the typing of the scripts.

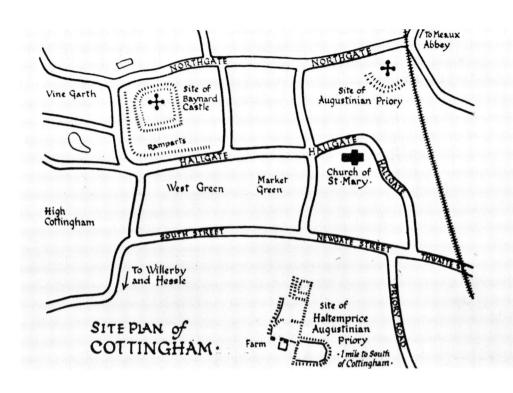

1. *Site plan of Cottingham.* The castle site and mound are all that remain of Baynard Castle, mentioned by John Leland in his tours of the county between 1530 and 1540. 'I saw wher Stutevilles Castelle, dobill dikid and motid, stoode of the which nothing now remaynith.' The Augustinian Priory founded by Thomas, second Lord Wake, was sited in Northgate near what is now Crossing Cottage, but owing to legal difficulties about the tenure of the land, the foundation was removed in 1324, two miles to the south and this is shown on the plan, adjacent to the modern Priory Road.

2. This view of the Church of St. Mary The Virgin is from a drawing by Thomas Spenceley in 1844. It shows the priests room formerly over the south porch and sundial set under the central window, both removed by the Reverend C. Overton in 1853 despite opposition in a vestry meeting held to decide on its fate.

3. A view of Hallgate looking east to the church dated about 1900. Many of the buildings and shops remain although in altered form. The chemist's shop with overhanging bay windows is still in its original form, and still functions in that role, but the adjacent property nearer the church was demolished around 1913 and two new shops erected, now a restaurant and a T.S. Bank.

4. Hallgate in the same area as the previous photograph but looking west, dated 1906. Near the left corner a pork butcher's shop (in operation in the 1970's), Cottingham's first post office, advertising 'Mazawattee Tea' and a barn with its gable end to the road. This barn is reputed to be the first registered meeting place for the Primitive Methodist congregation before the building of a church in neighbouring King Street (north) in 1860. Miss Lee had a wonderful toy shop in the block of shops further up the street, and a butcher's shop still remains in that role.

5. Mr. Knagg's general store and barber's shop, dated about 1910. Next door another barber, Richard Marshall, whose premises were to become the Midland Bank some three years later. The newspaper placards outside Mr. Knagg's shop record an all too common event — the loss of a Hull fishing trawler at sea. This shop was later to become Beals newsagency and remained in that family into the 1950's.

HALL GATE, COTTINGHAM.

6. This view of Hallgate, near to its junction with King Street (south), has changed to about 1922. The Midland Bank has moved into Richard Marshall's shop after amalgamation with the London Joint Stock Bank in 1913. A policeman is directing the rather sparse traffic at this time, although Cottingham was soon to be one of the earliest authorities to install traffic lights at this junction. Mr. Knagg's shop has been taken over by C.H. Beal and Tutill's millinery shop at the right hand edge of the picture is now Mr. Leonard Thompson's provision shop. Cussons of Hull have opened a similar shop on the opposite side of the road.

7. King Street (south) adjacent to Hallgate showing a group of young people in 1890. Note the very ornate gas lamp on the wall of a shop on the left hand side and the presence of two inns on the right hand side — The Tiger and The Angel. Further along out of sight the Duke of Cumberland. On the Market Green there are 'infill' buildings, which have been long demolished and on the far left can be seen the end of the stables belonging to Kingtree House. The fish shop at the mid-left with its door at an angle to the street is still there, but somewhat altered in its frontage.

8. *The Rectory* — a new rectory was built for the Reverend C. Overton in 1847 after he reported his previous house to be 'unsuitable'. It was built by William Richardson at a cost of £1,065 less £155 allowed for material from the old building. Ivyhouse in the church yard was bought in 1973 and shortly demolished to make way for a new rectory in 1974. The old rectory was demolished in 1976 and its elaborate portico erected in the new structure, some years before demolition of the old building.

9. *Ivy House*. This quaint house was built in the mid-eighteenth century; with rugged stone slate roof it stood in the church yard amidst the grave stones, until its demolition in 1974 to make way for the new rectory. It was occupied by Robert Garton in 1892 (he appears in the 1879 Kelly Directory at Southwood farm) and by 1905 Wm. Robinson, florist, was in residence. The house eventually passed to his unmarried daughters, the last inhabitants. One of these daughters had become a nurse in South Africa, but on retirement returned to live with her sister.

10. The so called old rectory in Hallgate, rebuilt and now occupied by a jeweller adjacent to Grandways supermarket. This is still recognisable thanks to the old sundial which was taken from the church porch when the priest room was removed in 1853 by Overton. There is no real evidence that the original building as shown was ever a rectory but it is possible that it was at some time used as the lodging of assistant priests or curates. This photograph was taken in 1956 shortly before rebuilding took place and it shows Mrs. L. Tranmer's sweet shop.

11. A general view of Hallgate from the King William IV inn showing some of the old shops on the right hand side of the picture. Mr. Frank Pullan's butchers shop is still there and owned by grandson Mr. Frank Pullan. The imposing shop on the left of this was Dixon's chemists shop. On the left of the picture is the King William IV inn, which is somewhat older than its bay window and beyond this the fenced yard of John Henry Wright, contractor and funeral director, followed by a dwelling known as Ivy Leigh and Mr. Houseley the sweep is shewn returning to his house. The date of this picture is probably between 1900 and 1906, the postmark being February 1905.

12. This postcard dates from about 1906, and shows the premises of Mr. John Henry Wright, mentioned in the previous picture. He demolished a part of the workshop in 1908 and erected a shop with a very elaborate flat for his family over the shop frontage. The post office moved at this time from its position near the church into Ivy Leigh and the notice case will be seen on the house wall. Mr. Wright is the figure near the notice case on the extreme right of the picture — he wears a billy-cock hat and has moustache and short beard. The second figure with billy-cock hat in the workshop yard is 'Cabby Kirby' who drove the horse cab to the railway station. The tall chimney in the background belongs to the brewery at the rear of the William IV inn.

13. The result of Mr. Wright's building is shown in this photograph of Mudd's shop, now moved into these premises from King Street (south). The entrance at the side leads to the builders yard, still known as 'Mudd's yard' and now leading to Mr. Stroud's shoe repairing workshop. The provision shop is now a confectioners.

14. A view of Hallgate looking west showing the result of these changes dated about 1912. A fine shop front has been built into Ivy Leigh which now houses the post office and the premises of the London Joint Stock Bank which amalgamated with the Midland Bank in 1913 and shortly afterwards moved to the corner of King Street (south) into its present situation. Sadly the very fine frontage of this building has been badly altered to accommodate other shops.

15. Beyond the King William IV premises across a narrow snicket we see here the premises of Ness and Company, corn dealers. To the rear of the building and recently demolished were the Maltings, comprising a malt store and kiln — these were part of the brewery undertaking run by William Thurloe, who was for a time also landlord of the inn. These maltings supplied the malt for the brewery at the rear of the inn next door. Ness' premises were purchased by Mr. Arthur Brocklesby in 1939 and rebuilt as a provision shop, subsequently on his retirement being converted into a garden shop. The maltings were totally demolished in 1977 to make way for a car park.

16. *The Maltings* were an important part of the history of brewing in Cottingham, comprising malt floor, store room and kiln. The malt floor was used as a reception room for weddings and social occasions for many years after the war owing to its great length. Falling into disuse it was demolished in 1977 to make way for a car park.

17. *Rydale* — this elegant town house has changed beyond recognition since the 1960's and is now the Cottingham branch of the Westminster Bank. The house was built in 1806 by Appleton Bennison of Hull.

HALLGATE. COTTINGHAM

18. *Hallgate Methodist Church* — built in 1878 to replace a Wesleyan foundation erected in Northgate in the early years of the nineteenth century. The old building in Northgate, built by Thomas Thompson, a friend of John Wesley, became a laundry and was demolished in the 1930's. The Hallgate church, although retaining its original exterior, has undergone extensive radical alterations to its interior. This view dates from the early 1920's.

19. *Applegarth* — sometimes known by this name — was actually situated on the site of the applegarth belonging to Baynard Castle. For many years a monumental mason's premises, it was demolished in the 1970's to make way for a complex of modern flats.

20. Entering a small private road at the west end of Hallgate on the right hand side, we pass a small Georgian house, to which are attached these stables and coach house. These belonged to the Throup family, famous for their breeding of hackney type carriage horses. Their future preservation is far from certain, owing to threat of development in the area.

21. The Manor house – this property is probably after the church, the most ancient of Cottingham buildings. Somewhat altered in recent years by the addition of a porch and gable on the left side and by interior modernisation, yet fundamentally it is a mid-sixteenth century timbered house sited on the mound of the Wake's Baynard Castle. Leland in his visit to Cottingham described it thus: 'At this present tyme be 4 sundry meane fermers houses, as one for eche of the 4 lordes, withyn the castelle garth,' a reference to the division of the manor into four parts on the marriage of the Holland heiresses. This photograph shows the building about 1890 in the possession of the Kirk family.

22. West Green about 1910 with the Blue Bell inn and a number of cottages surrounding the Green, many of which were demolished in the 1960's. The Blue Bell inn remains, although somewhat altered in line with modern ideas of 'restoration'. The cannon commemorates the Boer War; originally two in number, one was removed to the railway crossing in Thwaite Street. West Green marks the western limit of Hallgate and lies at its confluence with Finkle Street, Baynard Avenue, Dene Road (modern) and West End Road.

23. Opposite West Green and at the junction of Baynard Avenue and Dene road is Westfield House, formerly a fine Georgian house built by William Hall by 1778 on copyhold land of the Richmond manor. At one time occupied by the Grotrian family (associated with the Hull Daily Mail), which gave a corrupt form of the family name to the nearby Dene as Grote's Wood. During the two years 1937-1939 was used as a University Hall of residence until the outbreak of war. Since the war has sadly declined as a restaurant; the magnificent gardens have become a carpark, but a portion of the old arcaded garden wall remains flanking Dene Road. This view of house and garden dates from about 1910.

24. *The Grange* – situated on Harland Way, and built by George Knowsley, Hull merchant, about 1802 on a 9½ acre site copyhold of the Richmond manor. Knowsley carried out many extensive alterations to this area, closing the old path from Northgate to Hallgate through the castle grounds and opening George Street in lieu. He also resited Park Lane further east to extend his estate. Later occupied by the Ringroses, was derelict in the 1930's and demolished about 1937. Post war development of the site was the building of Cottingham High School and the conversion of the war-time camp site into the University campus. This photograph of the Grange dates about 1920.

25. *Click-em-in(n)*. This quaint old cottage situated on a slight bend at the entrance to Northgate stood on the edge of the old way through the castle grounds. Derelict for many years it has just been totally demolished and a new building is rising on the site, using the old bricks as a shell on the road facing side as a concession to 'conservation'. It has been romantically linked with the existence of a clandestine ale-house (it does not appear in directories), the last on the way to Beverley to speed the traveller on his way. Another legend connects this cottage with a practice of 'clicking-in' vagrants or tramps.

26. *Park House* — this house was copyhold, in part, of both Richmond and Sarum Manors and built for Alice Clegg, widow of Benjamin Clegg (possibly the dissenting Minister of that name). It is possibly the house shown on Jeffery's map of 1772. Eventually it passed to Thomas Wilson, Hull merchant, around 1848 and was converted into a mansion house. David Wilson was resident in the 1890's, a member of the ship owning family. In later years it became a private school and was demolished in 1935 to make way for the establishment of the King George Vth playing fields.

27. Northgate House (No. 150) This house, copyhold of the Sarum Manor, belonged to William Green, schoolmaster, in 1839 and to J.W. Burstall, Hull merchant in 1858. A variety of owners followed including the Ringroses and eventually the last owner was Dr. Arthur Tinley Sissons. This photograph shows the house and gardens facing north, with the former ballroom on the right later used as a schoolroom. Demolished in 1962; Dr. Sissons' name is remembered in the naming of the developed site as 'Tinley Close'.

28. This view of Northgate from the junction with King Street (north) dates from 1906 and shows the Cross Keys Inn in its old original frontage as part of a terrace block. By 1920 this was extensively altered to an appearance similar to its present form. The archway further along leads to Providence Place more popularly known as 'Sweep's Square', a small close of cottages. The shop was a general store and beer off-licence and until recent years functioned in this capacity, finally closing in the super-market era. The old Salvation Army hut can be seen by the second telegraph pole on the right hand side. It was totally destroyed by fire in 1958.

29. Raper's Garage about 1920. From humble beginnings grow large businesses! Motorists calling at this garage in present day Northgate would need a stretch of imagination to draw the connection between this photograph and the present 'serve yourself' emporium. Of great interest is the petrol sign advertising 'Russian Oil Products' (R.O.P.).

30. A small terrace of labourers cottages in Northgate, of interest in comparison with earlier examples of the houses of the gentry and also for a note on the back of the photograph stating that at one time 35 people lived in these simple two room cottages and that one woman 'took in washing' as a living.

31. North Mill — a combined wind and water mill, also known as Malt Mill and originally one of three water mills serving Cottingham. The water mill had its origin in mediaeval times, but the windmill built about 1821 was added to provide power when water was low. The mill was demolished in 1900, although it had existed for some time with only two sails in operation. Traces of the foundation and mill-race existed through the middle years of this century but disappeared on urbanisation of the area in the 1960's with the building of Mill Beck Lane and the partial enclosure of the beck. At the end of the 19th century the beck at this point was deep and wide enough to take a rowing boat, but the building of the waterworks in Millhouse Woods Lane eventually lowered the water table. This photograph was been dated 1884.

NORTH GATE, COTTINGHAM,   "SCOTT" SERIES. No. 690.

32. Cottages and Grey Stones, Northgate, with the entrance to North Mill and the beck on the left hand edge of the picture, dated 1903. The long low grey building in the centre background housed the fire engine newly purchased for Queen Victoria's Jubilee year 1887. Tom Boothby pictured on the driving seat of the fire engine in the next picture had a small holding and lived in the cottage adjacent to the beck (No. 50). Greystones (No. 46), building date unknown, but probably dating from the late eighteenth century, belonged to William Lee from at least 1807. It had a variety of owners and is now a nursing home for the elderly.

33. The Fire Engine 1887. Until the building of the Council Offices on Market Green in 1909 and the establishment of a fire station, the horse-drawn engines of which the 1887 model is shown, were kept in a variety of outhouses. This one housed in the east end of Northgate in an outbuilding shown in the previous picture. The engine was manned by a variety of people drawn from all walks of life in the village. The known members of this fire crew were: 1. 'Gassy' Wright, 2. Charles Gibson, 3. John Harrison, 4. Dr. Watson, 5. Tom Boothby (driver), 6. Tom Dales, 7. John Boynton, 8. Jim Fairbank, 9. Blacksmith Humble, 10. Tom Dales, 11. unknown, and 12. Billy Sipling.

34. New Village Road about 1920. At the turn of the eighteenth to nineteenth century the amount of poverty in Cottingham was great, and Thomas Thompson, a Hull banker and merchant, who lived at Cottingham, on hearing of a scheme in Nottingham for settling the poor on the land, decided to try a similar scheme. He persuaded the Overseers of the Poor to rent from the church eleven acres of land for £20 per annum. This was divided into ten strips at a nominal rent of two shillings per annum to selected poor in the area near Middledike Lane. Originally known as 'Paupers Gardens' this eventually became known as 'New Village'. Cottages were built by the tenants and only one of these remains on Endyke Lane.

35. One of the cottages on Endyke Lane from the New Village, about 1908, and as is usual with photographs of this date, plenty of children to provide human interest.

36. Returning to the main village via Thwaite Street we pass many of the houses of the gentry, and well to do merchants. This house, now a University Hall of Residence known as Holtby House, is of importance owing to its association with the Holtbys. It was the second home of Winifred Holtby the novelist and authoress of 'South Riding' and many other novels of local interest. Mrs. Alice Holtby was the first woman Alderman of the local county council and the model for Alderman Mrs. Beddows of 'South Riding'. The house was known as 'Bainesse' during their occupation, receiving its present name by association. This photograph shows the house in its original state during occupation by the Holtby's in the early 1930s.

Domino Cottages Thwaite St.

37. A view of Thwaite Street from the railway crossing dated about 1910 showing a group of cottages known locally for some unknown reason as 'Domino Cottages'. In the distance can be seen peeping over the high wall Charles Wilson's mansion inappropriately called 'The Bungalow'. Wilson was to become Lord Nunburnholme in later years in recognition of his success as a shipping magnate and had a much grander mansion known as Warter Priory. The farmhouse just visible at the extreme right disappeared in the 1960's to be replaced by flats and the Beechdale estate.

38. A view further along Thwaite Street showing the railway crossing with a steam train about to pass the signal cabin. The cannon is one of a pair from West Green, salvaged from the Boer War. Dated about 1910; it remained there until about 1934.

39. Looking down Thwaite Street from its junction with Snuff Mill Lane and Beck Bank. There are two inns – The Railway Inn and the Duke of York dated about 1910. A very early motorised tricycle is in evidence and a sign from one of the houses proclaims the existence of Tea Rooms.

40. Near the railway gates on the right hand side of Thwaite Street, looking in the direction of the gates, a driveway leads to Cottingham Hall, shown here at the turn of the century. Our thanks are due to Mrs. B. Worthington for permission to copy and reproduce this photograph from an original picture which she obtained from a relative in Manchester. As far as we are aware this is the only true photograph extant (together with a view of the other side of the house) of this important residence built by William Travis in 1795. According to Tickell it was one of the chief houses in Cottingham having an ornamental fish pond draining via a weir into the Beck. A path crossing the fish pond over a bridge led to the Snuff Mill. The Hall was demolished in 1935 to make way for housing development on Hall Walk and Mill Walk.

41. *The Snuff Mill* — originally one of the mediaeval corn mills of Cottingham on a lane adjoining Thwaite Street and Newgate Street. It was rebuilt by William Long of Driffield as a paper mill in 1722 until 1755 when William Travis, a tobacco merchant, used it as a snuff mill. William Travis built the elegant Millhouse which still stands about 1760. Later it was used successively by Samuel Bolton (1823) as a worsted mill and by Paley and Donkin later as an oil press cloth mill until 1904 when they moved to Station Road. The mill itself was later demolished leaving the Millhouse as a dwelling.

42. *Bridge House.* This small house described in contemporary records as 'a cottage or tenement' was acquired by Caius Thompson a Hull merchant, who probably rebuilt it. On his death it passed to his widow Mary in 1841. It probably passed to George Wells, merchant in 1851. Last occupied by Miss Fanny Foster, the house was demolished in 1935, but the grounds remain as a small garden on the corner of Beck Bank maintained by the local authority.

43. *Beck Bank Corner.* The buildings on this corner have been demolished (about 1961) and replaced by the new Railway Inn. A few of the old cottages along Beck Bank have been preserved. This photograph dates about 1910.

44. *Oakdene,* South Street was built by John Hill, Hull merchant, on a 9 acre site in 1816. He died in 1820 and was succeeded by his son John, a solicitor, although it was occupied by George Codd, town clerk of Hull, in the 1830's. The house was demolished in the 1960's to make way for a small housing estate named 'Oakdene' after the house. This photograph shows the house in the early 1930's.

45. *Southwood Hall, Burton Road,* the 17th century house of the Bacchus family was acquired by Samuel Watson, Hull merchant, in 1764. His widow Francis married the Reverend John Simpson of Bath who sold the house in 1811 to John Wray and it remained in the Wray family until 1867. It is possible that for a short time it was occupied by Thomas Thompson the Hull banker until the building of 'Cottingham Castle', although this is conjecture based on no great evidence. It is now encapsulated in a council house estate and has been in the Lazenby family for many years, having fortunately survived demolition. This view is dated about 1900.

CASTLE ROAD, COTTINGHAM

46. *Castle Road* leads to the Castle Hill Hospital and the entrance to the Hospital was formerly through the gateway shown in this picture of 1930. A part of the ornate entrance to Thomas Thompson's Victorian 'Gothick' Castle, it was wantonly demolished in the late 1960's on the basis that it obstructed entry to the hospital, despite the building of a new way in further up the road at a later date!

47. *Cottingham Castle*. In 1800 Thomas Thompson, Hull banker and shipping merchant, bought 54 acres of former open-field land, the result of the 1793 enclosures, and built a mansion there in 1814. It was built in the Victorian 'Gothick' style as a 'Castle'. Although there is no direct evidence that Thompson ever called it 'Cottingham Castle' the name was attached to the house and has caused confusion ever since, by comparison with the true Baynard Castle in Hallgate. The redoubtable General Thomas Perronet Thompson, son of the former who succeeded him in 1828, never lived independently at the house and whilst under tenancy, it was completely burned down in May 1861. The event is described in Overton's contemporary 'History of Cottingham'.

48. *The Reading Rooms* – this group of children dates from about 1939 and obviously represents some sort of fancy dress occasion. Situated in King Street (south) near the entrance to Finkle Street on the corner of Market Green, it dated from the mid-nineteenth century and was used as a general purpose recreational centre. It was demolished in the mid-1960's, together with a group of cottages and is now replaced by ornamental flower beds.

49. The old cottages and Sammy Green's blacksmith's shop on Market Green were demolished to make way for the new Council Offices which were officially opened in 1909. This picture shows the official opening by George Henry Watson, L.S.A., Medical Officer to the Urban District Council, seen here with his wife.

50. The old horse bus service to Hull was gradually replaced by the new motor bus in the early 1920's. This view of Market Green is dated about 1922 and shows one of the old solid tyred motor buses of the time, with the new Council Offices in the background.

KING STREET. COTTINGHAM

51. *The Duke of Cumberland* about 1922, with the cinema now appearing in Cottingham, as the 'Coliseum' on the right hand side of the picture, on the site of a group of cottages. This cinema was not long lived, the building became a button factory for a brief period and was then purchased by the Gas Company and converted into Gas Show Rooms, recently vacated. Again we see the old motor bus on its way into Hull, passing the 'Duke of Cumberland'.

52. At the beginning of this century Cottingham had five blacksmiths and Sammy Green worked at the forge on Market Green. On demolition of the forge he moved to King Street (north) corner (now Grandways) and was followed by Tom Gibson. Henry Humble had a forge in King Street (south), popularly known as Casson's yard, but humourously referred to as 'Leicester Square'!

53. This photograph of Thomas William Fawcett was taken on his last round in 1929. A public servant, known to all, he had completed 40 years of service to the post office.

54. Cottingham has always been noted as a centre for market gardening and this photograph shows the strawberry pickers at work in readiness for the Hull Market. The season was short and so as many pickers as possible were mustered including school children, given time off from school. This picture was taken in a field off Eppleworth Road about 1907.

55. *Newland Toll Bar.* This very old picture of early date shows the Toll House at the junction of Cottingham and Beverley Roads (Hull to Beverley) when Newland was in the parish of Cottingham. This toll house on the turnpike road was abolished in 1870 – the toll master was John French.

56. This view of George Street, named after George Knowsley, who created it to extend his estate around the Grange, is dated about 1910. The bread van is on its way down the centre of the street and away in the far right of the picture is the garden wall of the kitchen garden belonging to Park House on the other side of Northgate. For many years George Street survived change even after the war years, but of recent years all this is changing with some demolition, inbuilding, and 'conservation' which involves extensive alterations.

57. Hallgate House – this fine town house with impressive entrances on the Hallgate side and on its garden side facing Finkle Street, was built by John Wray in 1779 on land copyhold of the Richmond manor, purchased in 1769. It passed via various owners to Payne's, Hull solicitors, and eventually into the hands of the Hull Co-operative Society. It is now a Co-operative store on the ground floor and altered sadly beyond recognition.

58. Miss Harriet Boothby, attended by her father Tom, leaves No. 50 Northgate on 25th February 1915 for her marriage to John William Lawson. The bride travelled to St. Mary's Church in one of those 'new fangled motor-cars' — a great distinction when the usual mode of travel for weddings was via horse and carriage. The Lawson's lived in this cottage as cowkeepers and dairy farmers until its demolition in 1964. The land at the rear, which at the time of this photograph was a market garden, was developed as part of Mill Beck Lane, and Lawson Avenue, by 1970.

59. *Kingtree House* – another fine town house facing King Street (south), erected by Samuel Watson, Hull merchant, in the 1760's on land copyhold of the Rectory Manor. Arthur Young in his tours of the county described the grounds as 'well worth seeing'. It passed through a variety of hands, being last occupied by the Bilton family, some members being shown in this picture of the 1920's, of the east face, opening onto the gardens and tennis lawns. It was demolished in the 1960's to make way for shop development.

60. Cottingham was well served in early days by daily carriers to Hull and the advent of the motor-car saw the emergence of carriers and hauliers typified by this solid-tyred vehicle belonging to the Longbone family. This particular lorry dates from about 1922 and is well loaded with produce, probably for the Hull Market.

61. This view of Cottingham road near the Haworth Arms at Newland is very far removed from the urban development of the present day. It shows a blacksmith and wheelwright's shop near the old Haworth Arms, long replaced by a line of shops, Barclay's Bank and a new Haworth Arms. This is one of the oldest of view cards from this area, dated 1868, prepared by Edward Grocock under the pseudonym 'Egro'.

62. Five Arches, Eppleworth Road – a viaduct built in the 1880's on the Hull-Barnsley railway, crossed the parish of Cottingham at this point and for many years was a landmark to the traveller approaching Cottingham. In the face of much opposition it was demolished in November 1978, owing to the estimated colossal cost of preservation.

63. Mark Kirby School. Above the doorway of the schoolhouse, situated close by the south porch of the church, are the words 'Mark Kirby Free School A.D. 1712'. This is not correct, as Mark Kirby did not die until 1718 when the bequest for this school came into effect, but probably relates to his will of 1712. The school was situated next to the old workhouse (now replaced by the Church Hall) and was the subject of an action brought by William Hardy, schoolmaster in 1784, against the Overseers of the Poor who tried to eject him from the schoolhouse; 'they made public entry there in, chopping down the doors...' Mr. Hardy took his case to the courts at York and was awarded £600 in costs.

64. This tower on Castle Hill, often described locally as a look out tower, is one of the few remains of Thomas Thompson's Cottingham Castle. It was a folly of the type erected by the well-to-do gentry of the period, possibly used as a vantage point, but more of a status symbol. It is constructed of yellow brick, looking like stone and at the present time in a bad state of repair.

65. *The Avenue, Newgate Street* this view dates from 1910 and shows the entrance to the racing stables founded by Mr. Crowther Harrison in the first half of the 19th century as the 'Cottingham Stud'. In 1884 he handed over the stables to his son John Simons Harrison who carried it on for fifty years. One of his first yearlings of note was 'Merry Hampton', sold at Doncaster for 3,100 guineas. The first race in which this horse was entered was the Derby of 1887 which it won. A shoe of this horse was exhibited at the Local History Society's exhibition of 1953. The avenue was opened out in 1935 as King Tree Avenue when the land was developed. The building on the right of the picture is 'Shardeloes' built in the late 1880's and occupied by Waring Tothill in 1890.

66. Cottingham Water Works was built in 1890 at the head of Millhouse Woods Lane by Hull Corporation in search of additional water. The waterworks commenced modernisation in 1974, with removal of the old steam engines and their replacement with modern electric pumps. The boilers have been removed and the boiler room converted into a control room and office. The chimney was removed shortly afterwards, being in an unsafe condition.

67. There were three marine type engines by Worthington-Simpson installed in the tall engine house shown in the previous photograph. These engines were dated 1928 and two of them are shown in this photograph; their size may be judged by reference to the end wall brickwork. Two were removed in 1974, one remaining in situ for preservation, although not actively used. In later years, being obsolete, spares had to be made on the job when necessary.

68. 'The National United Order of Free Gardeners Friendly Society', established in 1820, provided a type of insurance against illness and loss of work, before the advent of the Social Services. The Cottingham Branch was known as the C.H. Wilson Lodge, and this photograph shows the officers about 1912 wearing their regalia. Standing, left to right: D. Dalby (saddler), W.E. Wright (gardener), G.C. Stevenson (gardener), Wm. Sipling (butcher), J.W. Hutton (green-grocer), C.W. Wright and son Edgar (joiners and undertakers), Moses Shores (coal merchant), A.H. Hardy (joiner), Th. Lyon (joiner) and Wm. Russell (builder). Seated: J.H. Whitehead (painter and decorator), C.H. Boynton (mill-foreman) and Ch.W. Ashton (plumber).

69. *Finkle Street* – 'the street with a bend in it' – a small street connecting King Street to West Green, which has undergone a great deal of change in the last two years after little change during the century. Here are some typical cottages, now all vanished and replaced by a complex of flats and shops.

70. One building still remains intact in Finkle Street, here seen as the police station about 1910 with a roster of six policemen. Cottingham now has no police station and no resident policeman and ironically the building is now a probation centre!

71. The Snuff Mill about 1900 in use by Paley and Donkin as a textile mill turning out press cloth for the Hull oil-pressing industry.

72. South Street from its junction with King Street about 1910 showing Mr. George Ashton's cycle and motor repair shop, later to become a garage and petrol station. Mr. R. Grantham, haulier and furniture remover, lived in the second cottage beyond this for many years until its demolition within the last two years. All this corner has been built up with flats recently.

73. Cottages formerly in South Street adjacent to Wellington House. These cottages were demolished in the 1960's to make way for development.

74. Fussey's Corner and Hallgate Farm — situated at the junction of Hallgate, Beck Bank and Station Road. This town farm was occupied by the Lawson Family, cow keepers and dairy farmers, at the turn of the century until about 1912 when they went to Townend Farm at Skidby. They were followed by Mr. Fussey who had recently purchased the bus service from Mr. Lazenby and he made this the starting point for his bus service to Hull, hence the popular name of 'Fussey's Corner'. This house was demolished in the 1960's after futile attempts to repair it. The land to the rear is now being developed in 1985. This photograph dates from about 1895.

75. This quiet country lane is West End Road at the turn of the century, long before the development of housing started in the 1930's. The road to the left in the middle distance is Eppleworth Road and West End Road leads into Northgate and Harland Way. Now this road is lined with houses, resembling many an urban way in the village.

76. The parish of Skidby was once part of the Cottingham parish and is Cottingham's nearest neighbour at a distance of two miles. This delightful rural scene is from the centre of the village near the church, showing a group of cottages containing the shop of Mr. Cargill who was also the postmaster. This view dates from the turn of the century and is far removed from the urban development which has taken place in the last ten years at Skidby. There are now extensive avenues and groups of modern houses to take the growing inflow of people returning each evening from their work in Hull and Beverley.